A Poet's Manifesto

Alexander Bentley

A Poet's Manifesto
Copyright © 2017 by Alexander Bentley

www.abentley.com

Edited by Sarah Doughty — who graciously
donated her time and editorial expertise.

Printed in the United States of America

First Printing, 2017

ISBN 978-0692937198

SOSII PRESS

Sun City, Arizona

To the best of the publisher's and author's knowledge, all
illustrations used in this book are of the public domain and do not
require attribution. If you are the original artist of an illustration, you
may contact the publisher to receive proper credit in a future printing
or to contest its inclusion.

The Fell Types are digitally reproduced by Igino Marini.
www.iginomarini.com

Alexander Bentley

Inkslinger. Wordsmith. Poet.

Discover more by the Author on Instagram,
Twitter and other social media outlets.

@abentleywrites

Dedicated to my godson,
Gaetano Raymond Vega

Never stop exploring.

TABLE OF CONTENTS

A Warning

You will never read poetry the same after finishing this book. This is a simple warning before you begin.

Every word of this manifesto was selected with intention and on purpose. The words are constructed into patterns and ordered in a precise manner — designed specifically to help you dive deeper into learning the ancient art of poetic composition and its highly powerful psychological influence.

If you want to admire poetry from an outsider's perspective or that of a traditional poet, then stop reading this book right now. Close the pages and don't read one more word.

You should turn back now before this book shatters your current beliefs and understanding of what poetry is. Do yourself a favor and take a poetry course at your local community college or university. You will be much safer there!

On the other hand, if you live dangerously, enjoy marvelous adventures or as the old cliché goes, *think outside the box*, then move forward and turn this book to the next page.

Behold! See for yourself what power words possess on the human mind.

INTRODUCTION

Dear Poets,

Our words hold power to change lives. Every line, every verse, every poem is a gateway into the reader's psyche. What we write next, if shared publicly, will find a reader who connects with our words and works.

We should live life for its enjoyment and write about those experiences, or, at least use those experiences as a reference point for our written works. A poet's past adds substance to the words and their meanings, creating a richer experience for the audience.

To some readers, our poems are a leisure enjoyment that brings intellectual fulfillment. But for others, our words are a balm for emotional healing. We are privileged to write and share with them all. Therefore, cherish your audience as much as they cherish your words of poetry.

Respectively,
Alexander Bentley
7th Sept. 2017

Manifesto

I. COMPOSITION
A Discourse on the Fine Art of Poetics

What is a poet?

A poet is a person who paints with words, forming a scene in the reader's mind. The scene progresses like a motion picture as lines are read and verses unfold. It is the duty of the poet to bring scenes and pictures to life, all within the most personal and private space on earth, the conscious mind of the reader.

The poet is like a madman who loves beauty. Only he sees what others cannot or dare not see. His vision is wildly imaginative and full of charged emotion.

This manifesto assumes you are a poet — amateur or professional — and that you want to shape your words into motion pictures of the mind. Even if it requires a bit of madness.

Words have a deep, lasting impression on the mind. Therefore, choose your words wisely!

Whatever you choose to write about: a person, place, object, event, memory or a feeling. Write about it with unfaltering passion, so the reader feels at one with your words. Writing should not be forced but should flow naturally, like water down a stream.

Words are keys that turn the tumblers inside the

conscious mind. Behind the locked door is a subconscious mind that remains dormant. Words, laid out as if they were lustrous pearls, beaded around one's consciousness, placed there by a poet's pen, lead to the awakening of the mind.

Certain combinations cause the mind to recall a distant memory, suddenly remember a smell from childhood, or associate them with a life experience. It's at this very moment you have captured the reader's attention. No, you've captured their entire mind. It's the next sequence of words that determine if you will hold their mind in complete and utter captivation.

The beauty of writing poetry is that you can write about a wide variety of topics. Many readers will relate to your words, but you won't know them personally or know what lost treasures their minds will dig up. You will speak to them so intimately they might call you a secret lover.

A poet shouldn't stop at intimacy, but consume the thoughts of the reader long after a single reading. Then, the poet is invited back into bed every time the reader desires that feeling of a sweet embrace. Stirring up these feelings is how the poet touches their mind, life, and ever searching soul.

A word is *more* than a word. It's a trigger. A potent device imbued with personal meaning.

Most people go their entire lives not realizing how powerful words are and which meanings are attached to them.

In the subconscious mind, a word translates into an icon. The icon, of either a word or phrase, goes through a process where it is searched, then matched against to its closest representation in a system I term, *the iconography of the mind* or *iconographic mind*. Much like a computer database, it is a repository of icon-information pairs. When an icon is matched, it unlocks, and the latest information activates in the subconscious mind.

As the subconscious mind sifts through the available information, individual bits make their way into the conscious mind. It is these snippets of information that begin to trigger other icons, repeating the process over again, all within a few milliseconds.

This rapid fire of information retrieval immediately causes a chemical reaction in the reader's brain and an emotional response.

Keywords in a sentence, usually nouns, or noun-verb pairs, trigger the icon translation and information retrieval.

A simple example of this is a chair. A chair is an object. We know the *why* and *how* people use chairs. A person will sit to rest the legs because that was the original design's intended purpose.

However, this information is only the first layer, the *base meaning*. More complex information is attached to the icon through a person's life experiences, conditionings, and education.

For each reader, the chair is more complicated than its base meaning, because it will unlock a specific memory.

The poet writes down the noun, chair. The reader sees the old, faded yellow chair he once sat on at the dinner table. As a kid, dinner was his favorite time of the day, because he ate his mother's home-cooked meals and spent quality time with his loving family.

Why did the chair leave such a powerful imprint on the reader's mind?

When he saw that faded yellow chair as he first approached the dining room, it meant a happy experience waited for him at the dinner table. He saw it every single evening after hearing his mother's voice call the family to eat dinner.

The mind associates nouns with events and experiences. These objects, people, and places are not static, but dynamic living instances in the slow-moving river of reality.

As the mind constantly thinks a new thought, it can be rooted in the past, present, or future. The goal of the poet, though this goal is usually unspoken, is to enter the reader's stream of consciousness. Penetration of this stream begins with the first line of a poem. How you open a poem will determine how you open a reader's mind.

For a moment, compare a poem to life and death. There is a beginning, or birth. There is a middle part where all the adventure happens, or life. Then, in the short blink of an eye, it's over, death. How a poem begins, continues, and ends reveals the poem's personality. Just like a person, a poem too can have a unique character. It's in this living persona where a reader finds an emotional connection.

The reader should be allowed the freedom to fill in the mundane details with their mind. The poet creates the framework and guides the direction of the narrative.

Crafting a Poem

Often, the title is equally as important as the poem itself, and should be treated with respect.

When writing a new poem, don't worry about giving it a title yet. Fall into the flow of writing the piece. Titling the poem should only come after completion. Never before.

In most cases, it's best to write the poem, and then return on a different occasion to set the poem's title. Space gives you distance, clarity, and fresh eyes for the task.

A poem's title should give the reader an idea of what the poem may be about or what subjects might be within the literary work. It should not reveal the climax but may allude to it in a subtle or cryptic language.

The Trials & Responsibilities of a Poet

A poet should let readers fill in many of the details with their active minds. A poet, like a great narrative writer, guides the flow of the motion picture show that unfolds in the mind's eye. She establishes a framework with a poem, which anchors the mind in a guided state of fixation. The poet wields much power with words, and for this reason, must control the narrative at all times to maintain balance.

The reader's mind is a wild lion and you are a courageous poet who must tame the king of the jungle, armed only with your words and gusto.

A poet does not need to be a walking dictionary to write great or profound poetry. All it takes is a heart, a pen and paper, and thoughts flowing like running ink. The words will end up where they will, automatically, without much decision-making.

Poetry itself is about feeling. The words are merely a medium to transfer this feeling from the writer who penned the words to the reader who reads the poem.

Later, the poet becomes the editor to do what they do best – edit! A poet would not be a poet if she were always editing as she wrote. One cannot write and edit at the same time. Two distinct cognitive processes are required. One process is creative, and the other, analytical.

When the time comes to edit your poem, you should read it through multiple times. Each time you read through, you should contemplate and consider what parts benefit the most from a revision. You may loop through multiple times as you go through this exercise. In the end, you will have a much stronger poem than when you began writing your first draft.

However, a poet's skills improve over time as she writes more poems and her writings mature in quality. Other ways a poet may improve her craft is by studying wisdom about the art form itself, as well as reading poems of other well-established poets.

If you want to become a better writer, a better poet, then you will be wise to read every day. But you don't need only to read poetry. Read books from authors and with words that have a different set of vocabulary. New words in your mind will trigger creativity. As a result, your poetry will indirectly benefit from your expanding library and diverse lexicon.

A poet is comparable to a computer programmer or hacker. Moving a person and a community and a nation. Moving and changing the literary world; even shaping the future of the world. With code designed to appear as text.

The reader's mind is always waiting to be stimulated. Boosted by something that holds its attention. The stimuli don't need to be much, but it does need to be entertaining, pleasing or captivating. Otherwise, you run the risk of losing the reader's attention.

If you know this fact and know the reader intentionally picked up your poem to read, wherever it may appear, then it gives you a greater advantage to hold their attention. Someone can show you a door, but it is you who must walk through it. The doorway is the reader's mind. When you knock, will you be invited in?

A true writer will write whether there's money or not. The likelihood of making a substantial living from writing is not likely. Therefore, it is better to abandon all hope that you will profit from your writings.

Instead, focus on putting all of your heart and

soul into your craft. Fuel your writings with passion — a passion for writing better than yesterday. Set out to make valuable contributions to the art of poetry and the success you deserve will follow.

Explore Uncomfortable Topics

As a poet, the failures of your life can be converted into poetic lines of text and shared with a wider readership. It is the personal life experiences that readers connect with. Everyone has struggled and failed at something. Therefore, most readers can relate to poems describing ventures that led to complete and utter failure.

You can use your failures as an opportunity to rise from the ashes, just like the mythical firebird, the Phoenix. Writing about these failures will connect you to the reader and inspire them to move beyond their struggle.

In this way, poetry serves as a therapeutic avenue that heals the soul and psyche from the damage of miserable and stressful experiences. To the reader, those failures start to become a distant memory, as the balm of your poems works its soothing comfort into the crevices and cracks of a broken, damaged self.

Not only is poetry a therapeutic experience for

the reader, but it is also your therapy. As the poet, it's your opportunity to exorcise the junk from your mind. To release the stuff that weighs you down, that binds you to the past. Let it go! Put it down on the page, free your mind from the past, then forget about the burdens that hold you back.

For this reason, I believe more people should read and write poetry. To free their souls and psyches from what burdens them.

Understanding & Dismissing Structured Writing

You can learn about poetic meter, measure, and form. However, these are of little value if it does not flow naturally from the reservoir of talent. Some poets and academics may disagree with the latter statement, but it is not the meter that puts pen to paper. Nor is it measure that ignites the flame within your heart to write. And the form is not shaped on paper alone, but first in your mind. You, the poet, mold the poem to your making and bring it to life!

Yes, it's beneficial to learn proper meter and form, but don't let them restrict your writing. Nor should you allow them to intimidate you, dampen your spirits and diminish your passion for writing.

To write good poetry, a poet need not have knowledge of poetic terminology. You don't need to know the difference between iamb and trochee or between an iambic pentameter and dactylic hexameter. As long as a poem walks and moves with its feet, you are following the right path.

The same goes for styles of poetry. You don't need to know the difference between a tanka or haiku, or between a limerick and a sonnet. It is best to write always from your heart, expanding your vocabulary as you improve your craft. What is meant to get written will be written.

Repetition: The techniques of alliteration, consonances, and assonance can be used to lull the reader into a dream-like state with the repetition of sounds and patterns.

Line Breaks: Where you break the line is significant, but where you do not is of greater importance.

The poet draws the line with a decision, making it turn one by one, as it leaves a powerful and lasting effect on the reader's mind.

A line is not a sentence. Punctuation, like a period, may fall in the middle of a line. When this happens, enjambment occurs. An enjambed line, or even stanza, typically causes the reader to put more effect on the final word of the line. It may also cause a person to speed from one line to the next, ignoring the line breaks to digest more of the poem, faster.

Rhythm: Another device the poet uses to cause the listening mind to enter a dream-like state is rhythm. When a poem establishes a rhythm, the reader expects it to continue. Cadence is good because it induces a natural state like that of a child drifting, back and forth on a playground swing.

Intentionally breaking rhythm is a powerful tool to draw the reader to a particular word or phrase. If the poet can cause this break *in rhythm* and *in line*, with a word full of charged meaning, then the poet causes the reader to have a profound emotional response.

Storytelling: A poet's strength comes from seeing ordinary everyday events in a new way. You must have the vision to see what others do not and write about them in such an eloquent fashion the reader feels what your poem is describing.

A poet should make the art of storytelling a part of her poems when the subject and style permit. The most common type, where storytelling shines brightly, is the narrative poem. But, it's possible to tell a story, or at least paint a scene from a story with most poem types. Look to the famously short

Japanese style known as haiku.

The best haiku poems capture a single passing moment in a small space on the page. Such a confined space places a lot of focus on making your story, your scene, and your moment as well-defined as possible.

A poet would do well to study the art of storytelling in more depth, even if there's no plan to write a formal short story or novel. Studying will help you, as the poet, learn to adequately describe the people, places, and things in greater detail, and enhance the reader's visualization of the poem.

Styles: Understand that we can lump a poem into one of two broad categories. A poem will either be a formal style, such as a sonnet or haiku, or a casual communicative style. The latter is like a free verse or an altered form of the former but written in a way that breaks from tradition.

What follows is an example from each category:

Formal Style - Haiku

Temple bells die out.
The fragrant blossoms remain.
A perfect evening!

This haiku poem by the legendary Matsuo Bashō follows the traditional 5-7-5 syllable format and runs its course over three lines.

Informal Style - Free Verse

Come slowly, Eden
Lips unused to thee.
Bashful, sip thy jasmines,
As the fainting bee,
Reaching late his flower,
Round her chamber hums,
Counts his nectars—alights,
And is lost in balms!

Emily Dickinson's short poem, "Come Slowly" is an example of free verse with two different rhyme-ending pairs. Emily, along with Walt Whitman, are oftentimes considered the mother and father of American free verse poetry.

Space: It's just as important what space you fill and what space you don't fill. A poet can use the principles of Feng Shui, employed with ink on paper, to maximize the emotional reaction sought from the reader.

Effect: The totality of effect is to determine the ending before you begin. A master poet will outline, in her mind or on paper, the end before writing a single line of a poem, and what the expected emotional reaction the reader must have. This type of forethought significantly betrays the notion that many poets are spontaneous with their works. Although inspiration may strike at any moment, it doesn't mean a poem finds completion after a single jotting across the page. It may take several revisions and drafts before the final version is ready for its audience.

Length: It's possible to compose long-form poetry by treating each verse as a small bite-sized poem. A poet can do this by perceiving each verse as a complete poem, that will stack with others later on in sequence.

When writing a long-form poem this way, it's important to remain consistent with the style, design and poetic meter. Of course, it's fine if some verses change slightly, as long as each verse builds upon the last one.

Whether you write long or short-form poetry is solely up to you. Just know writing longer poems shouldn't intimidate you, as you can tackle it and write it out in chunks.

The Where & How of Writing

A poet should have a sacred space where he or she feels comfortable writing poetry. In almost all circumstances, a poet will want a private place that is quiet and free of distractions. For the poet, writing is meditation.

On the contrary, it is important that the poet doesn't limit their writing to their space. They may choose to periodically go out into public spaces or nature to observe the environment. Either taking notes about what is seen or heard and later use this as material for composing a poem. Or, at other times, when inspiration strikes through observation, the poet may write a poem within the same environment.

A Conclusion on the Fine Art of Poetics

The power of poetic composition lies in the mind of the poet and demands transference to the fertile mind of the reader. There are no exceptions to this requisite.

A poem should stand on its own merit, as it can live and breathe long after it is written.

A poet speaks a universal truth that only the soul understands. The entire purpose of poetry is to speak to the soul of a person.

When you sit down to write poetry, destroy every thought you have about writing poetry. Philosophies and mechanical understanding of poetic craft have no right to be near a blank page. The rational brain will hinder creative flow.

A poet's words are forever. After everything else fades — the buildings, the heroes, the falling nations, civilization's accomplishments — the words of a poet vibrate through the universe, for eternity. The power of a single phrase, verse or poem lies in its unseen permanency.

People can destroy manuscripts and books of literature, like those destroyed with the Library of Alexandria. But a poet's words don't only live in the ethers after fire sets flame to page. No, a poet's words are incredibly powerful, and those words program the fabric of reality.

As a poet, you can communicate anything you want and have it absorbed by your audience's mind. But, only one question matters:

What will you write about today?

II. EDUCATION
A Discourse on Teaching the Art

This discourse on poetry education is filled with an ample supply of techniques that teachers can take and apply in the classroom. I must caution all teachers to first check with the proper authorities and decision-makers at your school, within your district or communities. Based on curriculum standards and policies you may not be able to add these lessons to your existing curriculum without approval.

Our schools teach students poetry, but a majority of our society has forgotten this ancient art form exists. I believe that's because most schools don't teach poetry correctly. Our education systems around the globe make it frustratingly difficult for young minds to fully grasp the beauty and mechanisms of this literary art.

If you are a teacher, you have the greatest opportunity to serve as an agent of change and influence the direction society takes.

Schools should never begin by having pupils read poems from the ever-growing grand corpus of poetry. No, instead, to connect a student with the poetic art, teachers must ask their students to pick a subject to write about and instruct the student to describe it in a few short lines.

Then this first poem is hidden, kept only for the student to read. The teacher will give the pupils the same exercise, but with a different subject. Again, the students hide their poems, not reading them in class. This exercise is repeated multiple times until each student has built confidence in their writing skills.

After about a week or two, for about 5-10 daily occurrences, the teacher can then introduce select poems from classics, either in one or two verses or the complete poem. However, the poem should be a relatively short one. The idea is to introduce the student to formal poetry and connect that reading experience with their writing experience. An approach like this is best done with short poems or a couple of verses.

Again, this is done for a short period of a couple of weeks. When the students are receptive, and these exercises and reading experiences hold the students' attention, then another exercise can be introduced.

This next exercise in the poetry curriculum is: a teacher picks a photograph and puts it up for all students to see. The pupils are instructed to write a short poem, in a few verses, about the subjects and scene captured in the assigned picture.

The students aren't asked to share their poems, but to keep them tucked away in their growing portfolio of poetry. Again, students will repeat this exercise for another 4-5 occurrences, to help the student build confidence in their writing abilities.

Where this exercise differs from the previous one is that the teacher finally asks the students to pick one of these poems and read it aloud to the class. The students get the chance to hear what the others are writing, but more importantly, it gives the young poet experience with public speaking and poetry recitals.

The image – the poem's subject – is placed at the front of the classroom. The reciting student's fellow peers should have their eyes anchored on the image a majority of the time during the recital. The image serves as a distraction and helps to minimize continuous eye contact placed on the presenter, which in turn builds that student's confidence while reducing anxiety.

Another way to help students learn how to write better poetry is to take classic and modern poems and ask the students to re-write the poem. But this method requires the student to look for words that are replaceable or lines that are best served by a re-write. The student is instructed to edit the text when they believe a better word choice is made present.

A teacher will instruct her class of pupils to choose one word, at a minimum, in each verse to replace. The substitution word may be any word as long as the student justifies the new choice.

When the students complete the exercise, each student will share with the teacher, and, if requested by the teacher, with the classmates.

An educational exercise such as this one not only helps a student write stronger lines, verses, and poems, it leads them to improve their editing skills. It does not mean the poem is ever perfect. It just adds a new tool to their literary skill set.

To help pupils write better descriptions in their poems, a student can highlight at least one of the five senses. For this next exercise a teacher can assign a particular out-of-classroom assignment. An out-of-classroom activity doesn't necessarily mean a homework assignment, but it does mean the students should leave the classroom or school campus, for a literary field trip. The reason is that the students will make observations in a public or natural setting and record down those observations on paper. The assignment works best as a field trip, where the teacher can supervise the students and answer any specific questions they may have.

The exercise goes like this: the teacher will advise the students they can only observe with one of the five senses and write a poem about it. For example, the teacher instructs her students to close their eyes and observe the environment with only their sense of hearing. After closing their eyes and silently listening for 5 to 10 minutes, then the student is asked to write a poem about the things they heard.

A student might say they heard water flowing down a stream, or birds chirping in a tree, or wind softly rustling leaves on a tree, or crickets in a distant field making noise. The possibilities are endless really, and each new environment means a different set of external cues.

A teacher will find particular environmental settings pair better with different senses. However, there's no wrong way to approach this exercise. But it is best to have the students practice with this writing prompt using two senses, of the five, at a minimum.

Here is another exercise. A student browses through a book, any book. The student scans the page until a particular word catches the attention of the eyes. A line of a verse is written using the eye-catching word. The student repeats this technique again, finding another word in the book and then writing a new line. A teacher can assign her students a set number of lines and verses for this exercise's poem.

Great poets carry with them a notebook — physical or electronic — to record thoughts as words. A real notebook with leafs of paper is most preferred, as it connects the writer to the roots of literacy. Regardless of the physical composition of the chosen instrument, it is highly important for a poet to have a means to jot down phrases, lines, and verses as it enters the mind.

A teacher can assign her students to carry around a notebook or a pad of paper with a writing instrument at all times. The students are then instructed to write down every single thought that comes to them, whether they form into a poem or just become ideas on paper. Students should complete this exercise for no less than a full week, as it will teach them the value of recording their thoughts.

Expanding the students' knowledge and experience with poetry is the purpose of educating them in this distinct and long-lasting literary genre.

This chapter was initially written to address a lagging educational system that has not fully fostered a well-rounded and well-designed curriculum for poetry. But you — as a parent, guardian or family member — may choose to incorporate any or all of these techniques and lessons into a learning environment at home. Don't wait for your child's school to take action.

I encourage all parents and guardians to pick up where their schools are lacking and give the gift of poetry to a child you love. Expand their young minds, literacy, and culture.

Imagine how many young lives can be touched by a concerted effort to teach young minds about poetry. Our world will rise to greater heights as a new cultural shift would be the direct result.

III. LANGUAGE
A Discourse on the Power of Human Languages

Language is the fundamental building block of consciousness, it is everywhere, in all things, simultaneously revealed yet hidden.

Scientists have discovered in the far reaches of space, on the outskirts, that the visible, detectable universe is made of binary code — zeros and ones. A digital language.

But language hits much closer to home. Coded into DNA — Deoxyribonucleic acid — is a unique language, where genetic material represents a packet of information. This code is understood by the cells to replicate, mutate or destroy. Transmitted in the genetic coding are detailed rules the cells must follow.

Whales sing their songs in the ocean while dolphins have unique acoustic signals they are able to transmit at long distances. Birds of the air have simple calls and complex songs, all which form the method of their communication. Even elephants, such as those in Central Africa and across many continents, possess a complex, mysterious language that scientists are still yet to decipher.

But language also lives inside our human minds,

as we vocalize our thoughts as speech and put down written markings on various mediums.

Words evoke emotions. Emotion provokes a response. A response is any action, verbal or non-verbal, small or large, mild or dramatic. When it comes down to it, emotions are chemical reactions in the brain that cause physical action.

It's important to understand the value of words and emotions, and how both intimately connect to one another. Language is beautiful, because of this symbiosis. What makes us uniquely human is the vast array of vocal sounds, their meanings and the emotions language shapes in our species.

Many ancient traditions across the globe, including the Egyptians, Greeks, and Indians, mention the high importance of language and the power of words. This knowledge should tell you language was valued by high-thinking societies long ago and continues to find value in modern culture.

Language is not power, but a tool for power. It is a force that a person wields for good or evil. Some people choose to deceive and manipulate with language while others use their words wisely for the benefit of community and society.

I can see where the misconception arises when we say "language is power." It happens because observers don't see it as a tool. It is often seen as a part of the person who is deemed powerful. Think great orators throughout history. If these individuals did not have a talent of charismatic speech, then they could not derive the power they were attributed with. Cut off their tongues and they have no speech to persuade.

Language does not determine the way you see the world. What you see in the world determines what you think about it and therefore what you speak, via language, about the observed.

How humans perceive the world is not influenced by language, but rather by the quality of the memories we remember.

There are people in this world who will attempt to persuade and manipulate others. You might be the receiving end of these deceivers. You may find yourself doing things you never thought you would find yourself doing otherwise. Without their influence. Most times this persuasion is done verbally, without physical aggression, and with deceptive, misleading words.

I believe it is the duty of poets, maybe not all of them, but a select few that want to turn over the tables of fate. And turn the tides of destiny to influence people to live a more promising and fulfilling future. This bold vision is possible with words, written or read out loud, in distinct patterns that unlock the true innate potential hidden within lost and deserving souls.

Our brain does not primarily think in language, but in icons. The symbols in our languages — whether in phonographic or logographic forms — are carriers for the icons. These icons represent what a person sees or discusses.

The most powerful sound in language is silence. In your poetry, give silence appropriate space on the page, and it will be converted to speech and thought.

When possible, use concrete language versus abstract words. This writing skill adds vivid clarity and depth to your poems. However, this shouldn't be a hard and fast rule. Sometimes a mix of concrete and abstract language can lure the reader deeper into your dramatic scenes and give them license to dream and feel.

Every language has its word roots that form into longer words. A majority of words are a combination of these word roots.

Seed words are a combination of letters, and they are put together to form word roots. In Sanskrit, which has an alphabet of fifty-two letters, these seed words are called *bija*.

People from many different Far Eastern religious and meditation practices are assigned a bija or power word to meditate upon by their guru. These can be phrases too. Traditionally, the meditator keeps this power word or phrase for life, as it was personally picked out for them based on their personality and behavioral tendencies.

A practitioner meditates upon a bija for the purpose of calming the mental faculties, increasing meditative focus and bypassing the conscious or active mind.

Although a poet can improve concentration and creativity by meditating, it's not mentioned here for that reason. Instead, it's raised here to draw your attention to how important the foundations of language are. People take words for granted, but a poet will value their worth and, therefore, understand their power.

A full discourse on linguistics and etymology is too much for these pages. But *etymology*, the study of word origins, is important for a poet to build a personal lexicon and understand the meaning of words chosen for one's poems. A quick and easy exercise is to look up every unfamiliar word in an etymological dictionary and pay careful attention to the word's origins, including the date it was introduced into culture, the roots that form it, and the development of its meaning.

A word today may mean something different than one or two decades ago, or drastically different from the time period and culture it originated.

The study of word origins is a powerful way to increase knowledge about the world, past, and present, and also of culture. As you may have observed, culture is not static and never will be. It is always changing and transforming.

That is why the art of poetry is necessary for a culture. Whether a poem is read from the page by a single reader or recited for an audience of more than one listener, it requires the undivided attention of the recipients.

Poets are servants of language and literature, weaving their thoughts, beliefs, and ideas into the social fabric of the collective.

Poetry has shaped humanity for millennia and will continue to do so long into the future, as long as language exists.

It is time to play your role as a modern-day poet and contribute to the collective body of literature that will influence current and future generations. You were born to breathe, bleed and write. Ink flows through your pulsing veins.

To get a better understanding of organic word formation, a poet should observe the sounds that infants and toddlers make as they begin to grow conscious of the language swirling around them. A boy or girl, who has yet to form or properly articulate a word, will make utterances that sound like words or at least noises that hold significance to that child. A baby deliberately utters ma-ma when he sees or wants his mother.

Iconographs triggered in the mind instantly produce a chemical reaction that traces along a specific pathway in the brain. Different images may cause chemicals to go down different paths depending on what response it triggers. This fact is why you get facial reactions from your listeners when you talk to them.

The power of words is that they create specific chemical processes to fire in the brain and then surface as emotional energy on the face and in the body as non-verbal cues and communication.

Remember that all words read or heard by a person must be converted from electrical signals and chemicals into something understood by the mind. The electrical impulses and chemical reactions are what happen in the brain and body. But what goes on in the brain and mind occurs in three distinct phases.

The three phases are chemical stimulation, neurological scanning, and mental matching. Only after each step in the process is completed will the human mind derive a meaning from the environmental stimulation (e.g. written words or speech).

The chemicals create a particular icon to be seen or recalled in the mind. Two paths will immediately follow after a physical chemical reaction causes images to appear in a person's mind. The iconographs are either converted into symbols and immediately next into language. Or the icons are translated by the mind into a base meaning, and a personal meaning if one exists. The order of the sequence depends on different variables, but the abstraction or complexity of an iconograph determines whether meaning comes before or after symbols and language.

A poem, from beginning to end, creates a feedback loop. Where the mind, with the brain's ongoing neurological support, continuously scans the iconographic database of the mind. It scans through the saved memories of events, knowledge, and information looking for a match to the symbols, language or language's theme.

Certain words via word suggestion can make a listener feel the effect of that word. For example, if you say "up" then the audience may feel uplifted or elated, at least, momentarily. If you say "down" the listener may feel low in spirit or deflated internally. As well, directional words like up, down, left, right, forward and backward may trigger non-verbal symptoms like a listener looking upward when you say the word, up, or feel a rising sensation.

Another example of word suggestion is the word "free" evoking a feeling of freedom or high spirits in the listener.

Language is a blessing, but also a curse. It is a blessing because it has allowed the human species to accomplish so much in the course of its evolutionary track and spread across far distances in a short time. It is a curse because we as individuals and as a collective still get into unnecessary conflicts. Many times these interpersonal conflicts exist due to a lack of understanding, poor word choice or the intentional use of words as weapons.

Language, as a tool, can impose a barrier to deriving meaning from language itself. All because a person uses language too much, thinking too deeply about what is being said or written on paper.

What if a sentient species living with perfect non-violent language, resulting in non-violent behavior, is the ultimate goal of life for the collective species? Perhaps this was the purpose for the invention of language in the first place. To minimize conflict and eliminate warring between tribes, nations and all people, all over the earth.

The visual subconscious came first before the linguistic subconscious mind, due to our evolutionary path. At the base primal level of homo sapiens, the visual sensory system is the bridge between the seen world and feelings. Therefore, emotions came long before language and higher analytical thinking.

It's important to understand that language, the body of words and norms, develops through a drifting effect over many decades and centuries. The change of a language happens below the level of consciousness, automatically through influences of its speakers and writers.

How a language develops, usually without much forethought means you – as a writer – consciously writing can wield an enormous amount of influence with your words, written or spoken, upon observing minds.

The power of speech must be felt, because we are socially emotional beings.

A poem read is not the real poem. It's merely an outer shell that contains the real power of the words within.

Words are the bridge between you and the reader. Language is what connects us. Without it, we wouldn't be where we are today.

IV. PERSUASION
A Discourse on Psychological Influence in Poetry

Once you are in a person's subconscious mind, you can go even deeper by using the various principles outlined in this manifesto.

All readers have desires. What they want determines what things they choose to make a part of their life. If you can tap into the most basic of human desires, you can easily connect and sway the emotional state of readers.

Understand that all people see the world through a mental filter. A person could be intelligent, but mental filters, imposed upon them, shape how they get, see and process information.

A poem is a type of mental filter, where you can transfer any information you want to the reader. Which happens within the confines of a few lines, verses or pages. Use all space on a page wisely to transmit information and feeling as you desire.

Just like desires, everyone has fears that we hold onto. And like desires, you can work core primal fears into a poem to elicit a distinct emotional reaction from a reader or listening audience.

For every fear, there is a desire. Keep this in mind when writing poems, as it gives you a psychographic understanding of your core target audience.

For example, death and dying are something everyone will experience indirectly and directly. Tied to thoughts of death and dying are the desire to either live longer, live healthier or enjoy life while alive. What kind of poem can you write based on these fears and desires?

A poet might be the most dangerous person in the world. Because, unlike politicians and actors, a poet can change a culture with a subtle poem or body of work. Think of the Beat Poets who influenced American culture during the 1950s and helped to shape beliefs well into the 1960s and beyond.

As a poet, you can introduce new ideas and beliefs into the minds of readers, and as a result into the stream of collective consciousness.

These newly introduced ideas and opinions can spread like wildfire, as good ones adhere to the true meaning of the word, meme. Memes are units of information that spread rapidly like a virus, and that shapes cultural beliefs and behavior with its wide distribution and penetration into consciousness.

Cascading is a poetic technique of layering objects or noun-verb pairs line by line to reveal a powerful truth, message or meaning. This technique can be done over the lines of a single verse or carried over many verses.

Additionally, you can cascade over many verses, revealing a deeper truth or meaning than what you shared in the first verse.

Here is a single-verse example from my own collection, which will be explained in greater detail in the Appendix accompanying this manifesto:

> *The window of pain*
> *is a broken glass,*
> *a shattered mess.*
> *I pick up the shards,*
> *sharp as knives.*
> *I cut myself*
> *to numb the pain.*
> *The pain —*
> *of losing you.*

A person has a cognitive mechanism that can be rightfully termed "mental flush." It's what the mind does when it quickly pulls up an image from the mind's iconographic database and then releases it from short-term memory.

The reason for this cognitive function is so it doesn't become fixated on the image for a long period, therefore becoming burdened by the energy required to keep it in memory.

However, this isn't always the case, because the

mind often dwells on things that excite or agitate it. When this happens, it holds that image or series of images in the mind until it becomes distracted or finds release from the mental picture's binding.

To bind a person's mind with a selected image or event, you can accomplish this by using the cascading technique.

A similar but equally useful poetic technique is *linking*. The poet applies this procedure when she takes words, phrases or themes in a poem, usually a long one, and repeats those elements, again and again, to drive home the meaning. The repetition doesn't need to be from line to line, as a poet would do with cascading. Instead, the poem contains these linking triggers or words throughout its body. Such as the very beginning and ending lines, or every other verse, as mere examples.

The repetition of the element itself, which causes the link in the reader's mind, is primarily thematic alliteration. Some readers will be easily lulled into a deeper state of entrancement while others will throw up a defensive mechanism to protect themselves. Don't fret though, because what you are going for is a memorable poem. To avoid this pitfall, carefully select the most impactful time to introduce it into one of your poems, and don't import the technique's usage it into every single poem you write.

Because people are analog and not binary, a poet can progressively induce a dream-like state until the words bypass the conscious mind entirely.

Everyone guards what is important and puts a priority on important things. You aren't a mind reader, but you can be a thought influencer. Since most humans have similar needs and desires, a poet can work these things into a poem's theme to influence belief and behavior.

When a reader becomes loyal to your works and seeks out new poems and books by you, then she becomes a true fan. You are now seen as an authority figure, even if that term isn't used, by that fan. These are the types of readers you want to keep as fans and supporting your work.

As well, it becomes easier to write for them, as you know the sort of themes your audience is receptive to and like. The lesson here is to listen to your fans, be responsive to any feedback they give and write a portion of poetry solely for them.

People are trying to persuade other people all the time. Rarely do they listen or have the time to focus on listening, because their mouths are moving, or their minds are running, rampantly with thoughts.

Yes, during the writing process you may spontaneously jot down a word. But at the first full reading after its composition, you should review and decide which words need to stay and which are replaceable with a quick edit. Editing is another way a poet's words become intentional; by deciding what you keep and why.

Psychographics is the personality, attitudes, and values of a person. It would also include their likes and dislikes and how those steer them toward and away from specific activities. Psychographics only makes up one aspect of a person or reader. For a deeper study, you may want to get familiar with demographics, geographics and behavioral analysis. The knowledge of all of these combined is the study and discipline of market segmentation.

Typically, market segmentation has been used to profile a buyer, so a company or advertising agency can target a particular segment of people. How would this be beneficial to a poet – especially a poet in the modern age? Because if you can understand your core audience along with different segments that may come across your poems and collections, then you can tailor the contents of your poetry to those groups. It does not mean you need to abandon your writing style and voice but can leverage insights from market segmentation to cover topics that relate to those specific segments.

Are poets comparable to sorcerers, casting spells on their audiences with carefully crafted strings of words? Poets just might be modern day magicians. If we look at the original meanings of the word, sorcerer, derives from Medieval Latin (sortiarius), meaning "teller of fortunes by lot." Also, it comes from the Latin genitive (sortis), which means "lot, fate, fortune." The same source word for sort or the act of sorting. A sorcerer is someone who sorts by influencing the future with abilities in the present. In today's world, most influence comes from media and media heavily uses language and symbols to wield influence on humans. Influencers persuade people to move, to think a certain way or take specific actions. How is this any different than what a medieval sorcerer did?

A *motif* is the most powerful element in literature. It is typically a noun, seen or unseen, but dominant and recurring. Edgar Allen Poe's raven plays a central role in his poem, The Raven. The black bird is a motif in Poe's work and one reason the poem itself is so memorable.

With a motif's introduction as the primary theme in a literary work and because it reoccurs from stanza to stanza or chapter to chapter, a reader walks away from the poem or story with the motif imprinted on their mind.

A motif is like the alliteration of a thematic element impressed upon the psyche. The beauty of a motif is that it waits in the mind, making a home there, until a moment of remembrance calls it forth from where it hides. But where else does it hide when it does not have a page to ride?

When the mind does not immediately recognize a word or image, then it acts much like a computer where it glitches out and returns no results. It then does one of two things: it goes into learning mode or tries to gloss over the meaning and details.

Sometimes introducing an unknown word or imagery into a poem and targeted at the right moment creates a state of induction or a deeper hypnotic trance.

Induction is the process that leads to a trance state. Hypnosis is a common tradition that uses induction, but trance-like states exist and are induced by other methods. Great music can induce a hypnotic trance. Swirling around in circles, like Sufi mystics practicing dhikr, can lead to a trance too. A well-written collection of poems can induce and entrance a reader for a long duration of time. All with the right words laid out in the right sequence for that person's psychographic profile.

People naturally want to be hypnotized so they can momentarily forget about their often mundane lives. The boredom and dissatisfaction of ordinary life is why people allow themselves to immerse their minds in a good book, or, they let themselves forget anything else exists when sitting in a theater watching a good movie.

The effectiveness of induction depends on the level of attention and concentration a person exerts. If someone is distracted and finds it difficult to read any words on a page, let alone your words, they won't be able to read more than a few lines or a stanza.

To get the full effect of induction you need the full attention of an individual. And if they are reading your works you won't be able to know otherwise. Therefore, write your poems as if you always have the full undivided attention of your reading audience.

Humans have a tendency to fill in the details with their minds. If a written piece is incomplete, uncomfortable or lacking in-depth descriptive language, then the person will make up the remaining details or base it on past experiences, sourced from memories.

Some of the best poems end up serving as a priming device to unlock memories from the unconscious mind. Priming is a technique to subliminally arouse a response from an individual without their conscious effort.

When research scientists flash words on a screen, for only a few milliseconds, then reintroduce those same words with a new set of words, that's an example of priming. The subject can more easily recall the first round of words versus the newer batch from the second set.

A poet can use priming by taking a single word, then periodically using and scattering it among the verses. An excellent example of priming is Edgar Allan Poe's "The Raven." Both the words "raven" and "nevermore" are distributed throughout the poem. A reader's mind becomes more acquainted with these two terms than any of the others.

Keywords in a poem serve as a cue that triggers memory recall in your brain's declarative or explicit memory system.

Memories go through a three step process: encoding, storing, and retrieving. The problem with memories is rarely with the storage of them unless there is a brain disorder or damaged region. The problem is in the encoding, which complicates the retrieval process. There can also be an issue with the retrieving not caused by how it was encoded. If there are no triggers or very few, then almost all people will have difficulty.

People who are vague in their descriptions of events make it much harder for an individual to recall a memory. A poet can aid a reader by using descriptive language, although the person may have never experienced the described event.

A graphic or vivid poem is beneficial to readers because it imprints itself onto the reader's memory. And a memorable poem seems to find a way to permeate itself into the collective consciousness. As reference, strong examples include Edgar Allan Poe's "The Raven" (Jan. 1844), Walt Whitman's "Leaves of Grass" (Jul. 1855) and Robert Frost's "The Road Not Taken" (Nov. 1916).

A poem's design on a page, whereby it leaves ample space where needed, creates a reading environment conducive to a reader-initiated mental collaboration. Based on this mental engagement, the act of reading poetry is a beautiful and meaningful collaboration between reader and poet.

Remember the rule of *relativism*: what a person perceives is determined by where they stand physically and what they understand mentally. But the breadth of understanding involves all the cognitive functions to come to a conclusion. However, a person may grossly misinterpret the state and condition of an object or thing and come to the wrong conclusion. Take advantage of a reader's understanding or lack thereof.

The art of suggestion is a strategy that only the best writers and poets can employ, as it requires pre-work, leading up to the subliminally suggested command. For example, I could write poems about a young boy who loves to read and talk about how reading has built his confidence when interacting with friends and strangers. I can paint this positive picture, with my words, highlighting the benefits of reading more. In fact, this can be done subtly by telling an overarching plot in a story or narrative poem.

I could add in keywords and phrases, like, "read," "reading," and "good reader." Here is a brief, but an exaggerated form of this method: He loved to read so much, he would read books to his classmates, and boy did they love to hear him read, just to listen to his voice say the words.

If this example were spread out over many pages of a book, a collection of poems, or even a novel, then my ultimate goal would be to manipulate the reader into reading more of my works. A writer can apply this method to any written form or media.

Gaining entry into a person's subconscious mind may hinge on the choice of your words. Particularly your choice of personal pronouns used in your poetics works.

Perspective Choices & Their Power

"You" and "we" are often a better choice than "I" or "I am," because the latter is more directly personal. Using "I" or "I am" could result in the conscious mind putting up a barrier as a direct means to defend itself from covert and overt command words.

There are poems that are designed to be blunt and straightforward, and these types require a sudden or forceful placement of words or phrases. A poem could start off mild, then work its way up quickly to an aggressive, in the reader's face, progression.

There are other pronouns that allow a poet to more quickly side-step a reader's conscious mind and find its way into the basement where the subconscious is. These pronouns include "he" or "him," "she" or "her," "they" or "them," and "we." In fact, pronouns comprise a secret language. Individuals who know how to wield the power of pronouns reign control over another person's mind and emotions.

"You" is a magical word, because it may indicate a singular "you" as in a very specific person, such as you – the reader – or the plural "you" as in a group of people. The listening mind, when it hears "you" will try to make a quick assessment to determine if "you" is plural or singular, compared to the surrounding syntax. It's for this reason that using "you" can momentarily disorient the reader, which allows you to side-step into the subconscious mind.

Due to its egocentric nature, a person's mind automatically thinks the usage of "you" is about the person observing (e.g. reading, listening) the word. This mental fault further aids a poet's ability in seizing control of a reader's mind. It's like talking directly to the reader.

The most powerful phrase, in any language, is "I love you." It is a linguistic feedback loop designed to stimulate an emotional response. What people give they expect in return. If a person gives love, then that person is awaiting a loving response back from the listener. Many other phrases create linguistic feedback loops, but "I love you" is by far the most powerful in all of existence.

The pronoun "we" holds much power, ranking next in order below "you." When a person uses "we" in their conversations, he can disarm the listener's conscious mind. The reason is simple: everyone wants to feel like they belong to a social group. Belonging to the right, or a desired, group creates a sense of pride and happiness within the individual.

A poet can take advantage of this pronoun by working "we" into the lines and stanzas of a poem. The reader, at least momentarily, will allow themselves to believe they belong in the same "we" group the author is addressing.

It is wise for a poet to continue learning about

grammar and linguistics, as a poet's power derives from their proper usage and sometimes intentional improper usage of words and phrases.

Phrasing and Word Choice

The power of direction can create a shift in feeling where the mind will go. For example, if I say, "the woman looked down from the cliff's edge," then you may have physically looked away and down from this book, or you had a sensation where you felt like you were going down. The other possibility is that you pictured a woman in your mind's eye metaphysically below your physical eyes. The latter result is to say you visualized a woman at a cliff's edge, but you projected this self-created imagery in your mind's eye at a small distance in front of your face and below your brow.

As a poet, you can use the power of direction to provoke specific emotional reactions from your readership or audience.

A descriptive language that uses "up," "rise" and "north" usually creates a positive feeling in the mind where "down," "descend" or "south" may evoke a negative emotion. It will depend on the context of the poem or storyline, as these two opposite directional-emotional pairs are reversible.

If the poem's context is describing a "sudden rush upward into the sky" this may evoke a sense of fear instead. The opposite would be "a slow, steady decline to a safe place." The latter usage of language most likely brings comfort to a reader rather than sadness or depression.

Increasing Impact

Even if a listener doesn't understand the meaning of a word or words, the speaker still imbues the words with power. Emotional energy from the speaker embeds itself in the words. If a person is confident when she speaks, it shows in her body language. But through tone, inflection, and pace, the energy is transferred. Essentially, the wavelengths of the phonetic sounds.

The pattern of syntax can lend an increase or decrease in power embedded in the words. A knowledgeable poet can structure his words in a way to fully energized a person reading his poem. Poetry that makes use of rhyme and rhythm aids the energization of the recipient.

There are multiple ways to build up energy. A poet can increase and decrease the energetic flow of words, much like a rollercoaster, to play on the mental and emotional energies required of the reader and his attentive mind.

A poet could slowly build up the energy to a climatic ending, or choose to start off strong but lower the energy until the reader feels drained and fatigued. The reason why a poet would do this is simple. Moving energy with words is done to match the context and meaning of stanzas and the overall poem.

Poetry may take advantage of color and its power. When a writing contains a color, the mind automatically visualizes that color as it remembers it. The color red will produce red imagery in the mind's eye, and each person will see a different hue of red. As well, individual red objects may pop into the person's mind. These objects, regardless of color, are a combination of memories where the person's mind remembers seeing those particular colored objects in the past. For example, when I say red, you may visualize a Stop sign or a red Corvette. An individual may see objects in their conscious mind because she remembers seeing a neighbor driving his Corvette in her childhood neighborhood, and never coming to a complete stop at the red "Stop" sign.

Colors are so influential that scientists have discovered color therapy, surprisingly, even works on blind people, physically and emotionally affecting their internal perception of the world.

A poet can leverage the reader's recognition of multiple senses in a single poem by using language that describes two or more senses. A poem may contain descriptions of what is seen (i.e. visual perception) and what is heard (i.e. auditory perception) as the narrator walks along a road that is not often traveled.

Or, if a poet dares, she may wish to employ *synesthesia* — a blending of the senses.

A brief example is:

The old woman,
trapped inside her house,
heard cats purring outside.

Their lullabies showered the sky,
in marvelous hues of blue —
But what she saw,
she knew was a lie.

V. CONTEMPLATION
A Discourse on Poetry's Mental Benefits

The art of poetry is simple:

Make the person feel.

A poem is a window into the soul. Peer into it, and you'll surprise yourself with what was previously unknown. As the poet, you discover a new part of your life force which remained hidden or out of reach. As the reader, reading a poem you did not write, you see a part that is foreign to you, yet familiar enough to be your own.

A lover of poetry comes to its pages because she is seeking something. She does not know what it is, but one thing is sure. She hopes to find it, or at least a glimpse, within the pages you have written.

This poetry aficionado is searching for the truth of her being. Always searching and slowly uncovering bits of truth, here and there. Waiting to find truth in the words and poems of the many different poets she reads.

Poetry is her therapy. It is her relief from what is ordinary and mundane about daily life. She is looking for greater meaning, a deeper purpose, and undeniable attraction. She wants to feel the extraordinary in the ordinary. And only the poet knows what she yearns for and how to give it to her. A poet speaks to her soul.

Every word in a poem should be intentional, as its meaning, meter or other contributing factors have an impact on the overall design and effects the reader's mind.

The moments where people fall into daydreams is the same mechanism used to lull a reader into a fantastical state of guided imagination.

Daydreaming happens when the mind de-focuses from one focal point of concentration and begins focusing on an internal thought or scene of imagery. This mechanism is valuable to the poet. A poet that can trigger this passive state of cognition will penetrate deeper into the reader's mind and guide the reader to experience deeper layers of thought and emotions not typically perceived.

Think of a poem as a guided meditation, where you want to describe enough of a scene to help the reader visualize what you want them to see. As well, adding more description to your poems ensures the reader feels the full emotional range you want them to undergo.

The induced dream-like state is why reading poetry is like a personal meditative journey.

The realization of the end brings momentary satisfaction or a letdown. You may feel let down because the end did not follow the potential alluded to in the beginning and middle. Or even what a person was hoping the entirety of the experience could have been.

The other let down scenario is that the whole experience was incredible and the person wishes it would not have ended when it did.

Satisfaction because the end lived up to everything the beginning and middle promised. There may have been a moment of complete awe at the end or a gradual build up to the climax.

How does this apply to poetry? It relates to the end-user experience and whether someone enjoys a poem or not. It determines if a person will read more poetry from that same author or if they will share your works with friends.

Readers always want to share good reads with others. It's no different with poetry. A reader will do this because the literary work made them feel and connect to a specific emotion — good or bad. It's the same reason why we buy ugly cars from incredibly talented salespeople — because the salesman made us feel something we don't always feel inside. Not only will the buyer purchase the vehicle, but they will tell all of their friends and family how much they loved the salesperson and car dealership.

Ultimately, when publishing poetry, in the end, it all comes down to how you made the reader feel, and how that feeling weaves itself into each reader's life.

The mind is a beast, and we must always feed it. It's always hungry, wanting more to eat. That's why it's hard for many people to meditate. And if they happen to meditate, then it's difficult to find an extended period of peace, since the hungry mind is impatient and quickly grows uneasy.

The poet can take advantage of this hungry mind by feeding it with words and scenes that are entertaining and pleasing.

Abstraction is healthy for the soul. Because of it, it allows the mind to dream and touch what it cannot see. But, as a poet, it is absolutely necessary for you to include at least one image or scene of imagery into your poem, to reinforce the visual cognitive capacities of the reader.

Not everyone can write poetry. And of those who write poetry, not all are good poets.

A poet is anyone who consistently writes poetry, either for enjoyment or publication. A poet is someone who applies the skill of writing and commits words to a page. A reader, on the other hand, is someone not skilled in writing, but enjoys it and appreciates the works of credible poets. Yes, a poet may read poems from other poets, but she perceives it differently than someone who doesn't write poetry.

This is the mind rule of appreciation versus application. Poets apply; readers appreciate.

Re-reading your poetry presents a feedback loop, as you often don't use the same mental mode as a writer to read poetry. Many writers, usually unintentionally, shift quickly into a reader's mindset, seeing the poem from an entirely different perspective. However, a poet is always closer to their work, so it's always best to have a trusted colleague or friend read new material and give their honest feedback.

What most people don't recognize is that emotions are not separate from the mind and cognitive function. Emotions are a part of the mind. Emotions are a reactive mode, which the mind takes to trigger actions in the body and further stimulate mental activity.

A poet can write precisely to a particular emotion. If you want to bring out a feeling of sadness in a reader, then word-paint a picture of sorrow. If you want to write about happiness, then describe a scene of gaiety and how it fills a person with joy.

When a poet writes a poem that touches on a negative emotion — hitting a nerve, so to speak — that poem allows the reader and her mind adequate space to quietly observe feelings created by it, then to gently let it go.

In this way, poetry is like a wide-eyed mindfulness meditation. The observer will react in a specific way, then be left to manage those emotions.

The emotions won't always be of a cynical nature but could be positive where the mind and body are expressing happiness, contentment or a state of inner peace.

VI. Reputation
A Discourse on Writing for Public Consumption

As a poet, you should respect those great poets who have come before you. If a person has talent in writing poetry, then you must pay them the proper respect, whether it be by public praise, through private admiration or supporting their work financially.

Each writer, and in turn, every poet, leaves behind a textual impression, in the corpus of literature, of who they are with their words.

Words do not lie. It is the person and feelings behind them that do. Words are so truthful that grammatical style, sentence composition, and word choice can reveal the nature and identity of a person.

Do not let public successes and praise of your poetical works distract you from perfecting your craft. You can always write better, but it must be done in solitude, not at workshops or discussing with friends, peers, and colleagues.

Building a body of work, that is worthy of greatness in the annals of literature takes time and must be done slowly, over many years and decades. A great poet does not only have one mesmerizing and memorable poem but has many outstanding writings attributed to their name. Long-term skilled writing is how artists with remarkable creative aptitude build up their reputation.

When writing poetry, don't worry about word counts or the length of your poetical works. Greatness does not come from quantity but rather the quality of your words.

Guard your reputation as a writer, because your words are a reflection of who you are. What you write and say in public can be used to pass judgment on you.

People will judge you or ignore you. You can't control what they say or do. You can only control how you choose to respond or not. As a writer, the only thing you have control over are your writings and what poetry you decide to publish.

At whatever cost, you should avoid the trappings of plagiarism. Don't give into the temptation of blatantly stealing the works of another writer, whether in whole or in part. It may seem like an easy thing to do and get away with. But if you're caught, and someone brings it to the public's eye, then your career, reputation and humanity are at stake. The consequences may be enormous, including a loss of your current fanbase, and possibly all of the future readers who would have discovered your works.

There's always an exception to the rule, where

some seemingly talented writers, who are actually thieves, do nothing but gain fans and followers. In their trajectory to fame, these pseudo-poets dramatically increase their book sales while passing off writings that don't belong to them. They can hide behind their shiny masks and fancy quotes, but they can't hide forever.

Eventually, the truth will come out, and they shall fall into the crosshairs of public scorn.

It's far more rewarding and beneficial to produce original content than to lose your entire reputation in a single devastating day.

From the poems you write and the books you publish, you will always find a varied degree of people who will write good and bad reviews about your works. Critics will be the harshest detractors and wield the widest influence. Learn to take the good with the bad, and focus on how you can improve your writings.

Other poets and writers can be critics, too. I feel like I should add that some poets let their "fame" go to their heads. These types of critics will use their success as a means of belittling other poets for their methods or choices. Undoubtedly, this is a negative reflection on them.

Critics might make a few valid points of your works, and it's wise to heed some of what they have to say. But do not invest too much emotional and mental energy on their critiques. Just take bits and pieces, seeing how you can use that information to make you a stronger writer.

A feedback loop applies to literary works as well, like novels, short stories, and poetry.

But what is the feedback loop? A *feedback loop* is a system that results in feedback from an action. If it is a positive loop, then the effect of the cause reinforces the action. When the result reinforces the loop, then it is most likely to occur again in the future.

If the loop is neutral, then there is a reasonable chance and high probability the action will continue even with neutral or zero feedback. One reason for this is because the doer of the measure sees a lack of feedback as acceptance of the cause and effect. Here is an example: a toddler may get into the kitchen cabinets and take out a few dishes and utensils, but the child's parent doesn't like this behavior. However, the parent is in the other room and doesn't see the mess until much later. Because there is no immediate feedback for the toddler's mischief, but neutral action, the child is not dissuaded from doing it again.

Now, the feedback most likely to thwart progress is the negative feedback loop. A system will find a way to minimize the adverse reaction, either through small adjustments or completely changing course. When this happens, the system will test the adjusted or new action and see what feedback results from the modification.

How is the feedback loop applied to poets? It's applicable because poetry is very much a social activity, as it requires both author and reader.

Feedback will come to a poet in multiple ways, including at recitals or spoken word events, from critics, reviewers and fans of a published work, as well as social media outlets.

My opinion is that social media provides a new or amateur poet the best feedback because it's nearly immediate. You post one of your poems or verses you've written. Then within seconds or minutes, you can see who's read it, liked it and left you a comment.

The more likes and comments you receive on social media, the more that feedback reinforces your creative spirit. The opposite could happen too, where a poet receives zero likes or comments. This type of feedback may hurt your feelings, especially if you thought your poem or verse was well written and enjoyable. You may have liked it, but others may have not liked it at all.

It's also worth noting that there are other factors involved. Like visibility, timing, etc. Learning to properly use Social Media is, in itself, almost as difficult as learning to write poetry.

Do not get discouraged when neutral, or possibly, negative feedback occurs. Re-read your post and know that that type of writing, style or subject may not work for you and your audience. Or that your fans and followers didn't see your latest Social Media offering.

Learn from the feedback loop and your writing career will benefit handsomely.

Find something that stands you apart from other poets. It can be your personality, themes you write about, how you interact with your core audience or your unique style of poetry. Whatever it is, turn up the volume to highlight this strength. Your unique brand helps to build your reputation and increase your overall readership.

My favorite author is Edgar Allan Poe. He had a number of gimmicks, whether intentional or stemming from his personality. He was rude in many circumstances, writing negative reviews about his peers who published, what he felt, cheap material.

Poe is also the godfather of the horror genre, established the detective genre even before there were real detectives in police forces around the globe, and one of the first authors to explore science fiction and fantasy with his short stories.

One other gimmick he used was creating

cryptographic puzzles that he challenged magazine readers to solve. Long before Dan Brown wrote The Da Vinci Code, Poe was weaving elaborate puzzles or cryptograms into his published stories.

Using gimmicks is not a necessary step for establishing an illustrious career. But if you want to make a lifelong career in writing and publishing poetry, then it can only benefit you to contrive a gimmick that is fitting of your personality and works.

Remember this advice. The world only knows what you have shared with them. This includes what is shared in private because there are many people out there who love to gossip and can't keep a secret if their life depended on it.

It's amazing the credibility one gains when they win an award from a respected organization. For example, the winner of the Walt Whitman Award almost always results in a bestselling book of the winning manuscript. One reason for this nearly immediate bestselling status is because the Academy of American Poets distributes the book widely through their organization to each associate-level member or above. Furthermore, the award itself in addition to the bestselling author status gives a combined effect that garners more attention.

But it's possible to build your reputation without awards or becoming a bestselling author. Ultimately, follow your heart and always strive for your aspirations. You might be the only person that supports your efforts. But it doesn't mean you should give up. Instead, do what you love and do what you believe is right for you.

Don't think because you write poetry you need to publish it. If you publish your poetry, don't believe that you need to become famous. Your heart knows its path; just be quiet long enough to listen to what it says. It'll guide you to where you need to go.

VII. LOGOMANCY
A Discourse on Charming with the Power of Words

A long time ago, there lived the Poets of the Powers — the Siddhars of India — who meditated incessantly, wrote moral and theistic poetry, and spoke magical utterances — both aloud and in silence. These ascetic poets practiced *logomancy* — or the divination art of words and speech.

This discourse on logomancy is the most advanced of this manifesto; therefore, tread lightly and take your time to digest the information herein. Beginner poets may not find this chapter immediately practical, but all of the teachings are worth learning about. In this way, you can discover the full extent that human language and poetry can afford you.

How the Senses Heighten Poetry

A poet who uses the power of the five senses in poetry makes it easier for a reader to connect with a poem. At a minimum, a poet should employ two of the five senses, in a poem that is three or more stanzas in length. Shorter poems may use less.

Think about reality and how you perceive your

world. You can see, hear, smell, taste, and touch. The two most common are seeing and hearing. The other three senses are not as common because it depends on the circumstances and what activities a person is doing.

Touch is the most powerful sense, as it's deeply rooted in our biology, as we first feel our mother's touch inside her womb and then after we are born. We also feel our mother's heartbeat, beating alongside our own.

A dominant force is exerted upon the reader's psyche when a poem describes the connection to these senses in detail.

Connecting stanzas or lines with other ones is a powerful trick to impress upon the reader's mind the significance of the event.

For example, you could write about a "soft wind gently touching my skin" in one stanza. Then in the next verse allude to how "the wind is like a lover's gentle heart" and how that person "entered my life." This method connects a beautiful metaphor with an event. The former stanza gives strength to the latter.

The five great, or base, elements originate in Eastern spiritual and religious philosophy. The *five elements* are earth, water, fire, wind, and ether. A poet can work these base elements, or the derivatives of these elements, into a poem.

All five of these elements are innately known to the reader, as they make up the physical world. Weaving them into a poem makes it believable, as a poet is describing something tangible and familiar.

These five significant elements tie back to the five senses. Hearing relates to the element of ether, as it is the medium in which sounds pass through. The Wind, or Air, correlates to the sense of touch. Fire, a manifestation of light, relates to seeing, or vision. Water is deeply connected to taste, because if the tongue becomes sickened and lacks proper hydration, then it loses its tasting ability. Earth is related to smell, as all good smelling things come from nature. As well, bad smelling things, like feces and corpses return to the earth.

The Power of Predispositions

According to ancient Eastern tradition, it is said every person has encountered temptation by one of nine physical pathways, or gates. Not only that, but temptation can lead to obsession and addiction.

A poet may do well to write a poem that describes at least one temptation derived from opening a seal on any one of *Nine Gates of Destruction*. These gates include the three pairs: eyes, ears, nostrils. As well, the three remaining gates and the single entry points are the mouth, sexual organs, and anus.

Furthermore, the Nine Gates of Destruction make up only one link on a chain of eighteen binding predispositions. What Eastern tradition calls the *Eighteen Links of Bondage*. Every human is bound to at least one or more links in the chain that binds all of humanity.

A person's fixation on any one of the eighteen, for extended amounts of time, results in predisposition, dependency or destruction. Where you focus your attention is where your energy goes. What you focus on is what takes hold of your mind.

Bondage can begin with the three states of time: Past (1), Present (2), Future (3). If a person has unpaid debts or secrets they wish to escape, they are bound to moments of time that lie behind them. Their mind will dwell not in the current moment, nor dream about a future life, but always be drawn to what is in the Past.

When a person possesses anxiety about what events are yet to come or experiences that will never happen, then it is said that person is bound to the Future.

The destruction of the Present happens when a person worries incessantly about the Past or Future, or even when she is unable to cope with a crisis in the current moment.

The next two links in the chain constitute the dual nature of a human: Body (4) and Mind (5). There are times when our Body feels lazy and is unwilling to move, but our Mind is highly active with a thousand thoughts. Or, the Mind is fatigued, but the Body is full of vital energy.

The Body is like a City with Nine Gates that lead to destruction, whereby a person is tempted to travel down one of many destructive paths. This predisposition also includes health concerns and apparent illnesses.

If someone is bound to a mental illness or exhibits skewed mental filters, then they have an inclination of the Mind. A skewed mental filter is the type of belief that does not stem from verifiable facts in reality. Beliefs, whether fact or fiction, play a powerful role in swaying individuals and groups to speak and act in specific ways that only further strengthen the belief.

When a person is worried about the aging of the Body or Mind, then there is a predisposition toward Life (6). Life's polar opposite is death. Poems that explore this theme plays to this predisposition.

Individuals who have money problems, desire prosperity or have an obsession with getting rich are the types of people who are predisposed toward Wealth (7). When money is the focus of their life, it skews their perception of the world and can quite possibly lead to their destructive undoing.

A person that continually seeks a higher position in life or who falls into the traps of peer pressure and social status is someone bound to the link of Substance (8). When this predisposition is maximized to the extreme, individuals will act out in ways to garner the attention and praise they seek.

Someone who is more concerned about themselves more than others and displays egotistic behavior is someone bound to the link of Self-Regard (9). Narcissistic personalities are tightly bound by this link in the chain.

A person who intentionally looks for opportunities, even to the extent where they may look foolish when falling for scams is someone who is bound to the link of Gold (10).

I once met an elderly woman who fell for a scam. She was contacted on the phone by a scammer that said she inherited a mysterious wood chest. The person on the other line convinced her it was filled with gold, since it was so heavy. The scammer said it wasn't possible to view the contents, because it was locked securely. But the man was willing to ship the chest via freight, if the woman only made a wire payment of $10,000.

The woman happily paid. Not once, but twice

when the scammer told her the freight company said it would cost an additional $10,000 — a total of $20,000 — to ship the "inherited" wood chest to the United States from Nigeria. To say the least, she was emotionally and physically devastated to learn she was scammed, never to see the chest that possibly contained millions of dollars in gold or her life savings she wired to a stranger.

The next predisposition is one that stimulates a sense of belonging. Someone who is security-minded putting home life, their social circle and country above most priorities in life is a person bound to the Land (11). These types of personalities might be labeled patriotic and possess a nationalist fervor.

When a man or woman intentionally seeks and needs companionship from another human being, that is a sign he or she is bound by the link of Romance (12). Love poems are very popular for a reason, especially amongst a female readership. Subtly, throughout our entire lives, this predisposition is driven by the love and affection we received from our mothers at an early age.

The tendency of feeling passionate about projects or putting the cart before the horse is a person filled with Lust (13), and bound by it. A person with this tendency does not think before they act, or at least act without having all of the facts. It is interesting to note how Lust pollutes the Mind and projects a skewed mental filter over an individual's rational and analytical brain.

The other emotions that complete the Eighteen Links of Bondage include Anger (14), Greed (15), Infatuation (16), Pride (17), and Envy (18). These emotions constitute the *Five Emotions of Clouded Judgment*, resulting in a hectic mental life.

If you want to write a great poem, then you should write about one or more of these predispositions. If the reader isn't predisposed to the theme written about in your poem, then she almost definitely knows a person that is. In this way, she will connect with your composition indirectly. Otherwise, if she does have one of the eighteen predispositions, then your words will speak directly to her and therefore enchant her in the process of reading.

The Esoteric Nature of Words

A word is like a seed, not only because it gets planted in the fertile ground of a listener's mind. It is also like a seed because it has a shell. That's the outer layer, which is most commonly heard by an audience when it is pronounced. Behind the vibrations that form the outer layer is the inner. Inside is the energy that gives life to the vibrations. This power derives from within the ethers, and the words travel through this elemental medium.

The true power of a word depends on the listening mind's understanding of the word. If the mind doesn't discern a meaning, then there's no power over the listener. Look at foreign language learners that don't know a single word prior to translation. The learners at first aren't able to discern meaning from the language spoken.

Be forewarned, that in language contexts in which a word meaning is unknown, that word still carries power within it. Phonetically a word contains power from its energetic impression. Think of a word's pronunciation. Some words catch our ears more than others. These words sound fascinating compared to how other words might sound.

As well, words become empowered by the speaker's tone and inflection. Any word can be said forcefully in an aggressive manner or calmly in a peaceful way. The energy between these two dramatically different scenarios is heard and felt by listeners.

Although it's outside the realm of written poetry when a person says a word or sentence that individual transmits emotional energy through their face and body. Words are this powerful that it profoundly affects a speaker. In return, when a listener experiences words, that person sees, hears and feels the words.

The fact that a word or phrase carries emotional energy with it is an important distinction of language. Whatever medium communication transmits through, audible or visual, a person experiences words. An audience doesn't just see or hear words; the words are encountered. It becomes a personal experience due to the stimulation and reactive process that occurs within the brain.

Objects may also contain the energetic fingerprints of a word or phrase. Historically, amulets, pendants, talismans and coins have been used to inscribe words upon their surfaces and imbue the object with power. The object was often carried on or worn by the owner for protection or luck.

A poem written on a leaf of paper is an object and is one of the best mediums in the world to carry the power of words. The words themselves, on objects, when read aloud or silently by someone other than the owner, will have an immediate psychological effect on that individual. Besides, the owner of the object reaps the psychological benefit of confidence, as they believe the object brings them good luck or helps them avoid bad luck.

Items with words, when used by the owner for protection, luck or influence, are merely a *placebo*. A placebo is any substance, procedure or material, which is harmless in nature, used as a measure to control and afford a psychological benefit. The placebo effect is powerful, and this is a real example of its mental and emotional benefits. If a person's belief is strong enough, they will bring good fortune upon themselves. At a minimum, the word empowered object may reduce or neutralize negative thoughts.

But objects with words may have both powerful psychological and physiological effect on the observer. These benefits only happen if the person can read the words or phrase and understand the meaning. If the observer discerns no meaning, then no power is cast over their mind and body. For this reason, ancient amulets and talismans often evoked a religious belief, as to play on the fears of religious adherents and sect members.

Ideas, Beliefs & Sleight-of-Mind

Belief systems are powerful allies to a poet, as a poem can play for or against a particular view. If a poet wants to evoke fear in his readers, then all it takes is to amplify the belief that supports that fear. If a poet wants to cause an audience to get angry, then he could attack any single idea. If done correctly, the result would be a total uproar!

In fact, this same method of amplifying or attacking beliefs has been used in the past, either accidentally or deliberately, by the mainstream media and public figures to misdirect audiences, hide important facts and sway public opinion. All of this falls into the Sleight-of-Mind category.

When it comes down to it, magic is the use of thought-energy and word-energy to bring your desires into reality. A person may use the power of thoughts, words and mind manipulation for internal development or external manifestation.

Magic may be unorthodox, especially as it gets into strange methods, but a prayer is an ancient form of magic, as it strives to manifest our thoughts of desire into a physically, tangible outcome.

Symbolism is the foundation of magical practices. Symbols are at the core of written languages. The observer cannot discern unknown symbols, but they still may have a subtle emotional effect on a person. Some people are immune to symbols used for magic, even under the ritual of a master.

This manifesto is not a religious discourse, but I must veer into the realm of religious lore, just for a short period of time.

Throughout our remembered history, thousands

of gods have been worshipped by people of many different religions. One god of note – the Judeo-Christian god – is rumored to have seventy-two different names, constructed into sigil form out of the Hebrew language. Some Jewish devotees and scholars may claim the letters of the Hebrew language were birthed into existence only after God breathed life into each holy name. It is claimed these seventy-two names grant the speaker over three hundred powers, and esoteric magicians and kabbalists report an archangel guards each sigil.

These teachings, never substantiated by fact, explain the most powerful word in the universe is the name of the Judeo-Christian god. One theory holds the original holy name contains the same audible frequency that brought the universe into existence. The claims are that this limitless vibrational power was the originating force behind the universal big bang event.

If this myth is true, then it means the possibility exists that a word so powerful was once known, at least by a few select individuals. Maybe those elite were true poets of power.

But don't get your hopes too high, as the hunt for this holy name could result in a person wasting their entire life, trying to turn up the treasure without luck. Maybe because it's all a Sleight-of-Mind trick, orchestrated to convince you that the religious elite and their god have power.

Symbols, Sigils & Sorcery

A sigil is a sign or symbol, whether painted, engraved or written, that purportedly carries magical powers. Sigil is a word derived from Latin and means "seal." Other magical devices include runestones and crests, which rightfully are works of art.

The key differentiator between a regular work of art and a magical work of art is that specific intent is used to energize the creative work. A poet can use sigils in poetry as well, as long as she sets out in the beginning with this purpose in mind. She does this by intentionally writing a poem that seeks to provoke a particular reaction or result from its audience or program the universe to deliver the desired outcome.

The chaos magic technique of sigilization takes words or phrases, then eliminates specific characters, usually the vowels, to reduce it to a base form. The magician switches all of the letters around so no words can be detected. From here, the practitioner of magic concentrates on the letters in their new form and creates a custom-made symbol representing the energy of those letters. This modern usage of sigils was popularized by Austin Osman Spare, an English-born occultist and painter from London.

The same process applies to poetry, where the poet comes up with a narrative or outlines a concept, then eliminates unnecessary or unwanted elements. From here, the poet would write a stanza or poem that masks the real intent and purpose of the written work but allows the reader to fall under its spell.

One example that parallels the original sigil technique is to write a phrase of what you want the future to be like for you. Then, remove all vowels from the words. Only consonants remain. Next, jumble the letters to obfuscate their original placement. Finally, lay out the letters in the same order vertically from top to bottom, down the page. In your poem, each line will start with a word that matches that line's letter.

One variation of this sigilization technique includes taking a whole phrase, without removing the vowels or scattering the letters, and writing an entire poem with these words covertly seeded throughout the text. Optionally, you may capitalize the first letter of each word, as to draw the reader's eyes to those specific words. However, adding this option to your sigil may lead to the discovery of your phrase. A less magical, yet far superior way to hide context and codes in language is through the use of ciphers, which Edgar Allan Poe challenged readers to solve.

Another famous poet, although history sees him more as a seer than a poet, may have dabbled in magic. It is quite possible that 16th-century French physician and reputed prophet Michel de Nostredame (Latinized: Nostradamus) used a highly sophisticated sigil technique to compose hundreds of four-line poems (i.e. quatrains). His technique concealed the true meaning of his poetic writings, which was warranted during highly dangerous and political times.

If you are a poet or a person who is comfortable dabbling in magic, then I will reveal to you a more advanced version of sigilization.

In this technique, you write out a very specific affirmation, where you include many nouns, such as people you admire, places you want to visit, things you want to possess, or dreams you want to accomplish. You will take each of these nouns and obscure its true meaning, isolating it strictly to the object, detached of the meaning related to your phrase. Then, you write a poem embedded with icons representing these nouns. The icons should not reveal a clear meaning or correlation to your intention. If you choose, some nouns can stay as is, without converting to a representative image.

To convey what I mean, it is best I share a brief, but highly powerful example.

Let's say we have this phrase, "Before I die, I want to ride horses, visit the U.S. President at the White House, and travel the world." We can then convert this phrase into a powerful, allegorical poem:

Moving swiftly through my dreams
On a chariot, I'm pulled by horses
Riding through the black doors of Death
I escape the Dark Reaper's touch
I find myself in the courtyard of the King
Greeted by a White Wizard's clutch
He tells me to "Go! Travel the Seven Seas —
to escape Karma's bitter grudge!"

This advanced form of sigilization, whereby blending the art of poetry with the art of magic, is known as *Sigillum Poetica*.

VIII. Final Words
The End of the Seven Discourses

Energy radiates from the core of our being, from every living cell in our body, even when we are at rest. It is this power that seeks to move and animate reality, to bring form to the world.

From the deepest parts of our being, our consciousness flows outward. This energy may begin as a thought in our mind but later manifests in speech or as a deed. How we control this power controls the course of our life:

What we think, we become.
What we speak, we see.

At least, that is the premise of how reality manifests, from inside all living things, outwardly affecting other living and non-living things. But what we think may not always come into existence. This situation happens because we are not devoting enough speech-energy and action-energy to support our thought-energy, and to bring our desires to life.

Only through belief, willpower and persistence can we can transfer our energy and thoughts into the fabric of reality. I mention this conclusion, based on many years of meditating and soul searching. During my younger years, I delved into a wide variety of spiritual traditions, religious ideologies, and ancient philosophies.

But as I grow older in age, I see that all my experiences have led me to this moment – to write this manifesto and for you to read it. I firmly believe our paths have crossed so I may share my knowledge with you and to awaken the magic of poetry within your heart.

May your life and the lives of future generations receive this wisdom and learn the beauty of the grand poetic mystery. From this knowledge, let us all make poetry dance elegantly in the motion picture of the One Collective Mind.

"All things arise in unison. Thereby we see their return."
– Lao Tzu, author of Tao Te Ching

APPENDIX

A THEORY OF POETRY & PSYCHOLOGY

What is a poem?

It's a string of words — a code — that instantly implants itself in the reader's mind. Like beautifully written computer code, a poem can trigger certain processes in the operating system of the mind. A poem can provoke emotions and memories to swell up in the reader, unexpectedly and without apology. A love poem might pull on one's heartstrings or a dark poem, like the ones written by Edgar Allan Poe, can force us to look at our deepest, darkest secrets.

Whatever the poem, we as readers internalize it. The mind instantly searches in its database of collected experiences to see if we can relate. Haven't you read poetry before and related to it so well that you thought the poet was writing about an event from your life experience?

I believe poetry goes deeper than this. It starts with the words you read as you read them, even before the mind can piece together the meaning of the lines and verses. What do I mean?

Back in 2015, I posted a short poem I wrote to my Instagram page. The poem is titled, "Window of Pain." It's a favorite example of mine to explain my theory of poetry and psychology. The poem reads:

The window of pain
is a broken glass,
a shattered mess.
I pick up the shards,
sharp as knives.
I cut myself
to numb the pain.
The pain —
of losing you.

This example strengthens my theory because this short poem contains a design with purpose. Yes, the feelings behind it are real, but it was written in such a way to provoke your darkest emotions. Let's start at the beginning and see why.

The first line reads, "The window of pain."

There are two key words in this line: window and pain. With window, your mind will automatically, due to thousands of years of evolutionary and linguistic conditioning, associate the thousands of memory-images of windows you've seen in your lifetime.

Furthermore, any time a person uses a word, and you aren't viewing the object it describes, your mind automatically creates an image of that object. Over time this object-image becomes the common static image your brain uses for that particular object.

Think for a moment, go deep into your mind, and think clearly what a window looks like to you.

Is the window open or covered with glass? If the window is made of glass, how many panes of glass does it have? Can you see the structure of the crossbeams that hold the glass panels in place?

If you research windows, you'll see there are many different types of windows. But based on all your past experiences of seeing windows, your mind will automatically visualize its perfect common static image for a window. The mind does this quickly, in less than a second, when it hears or reads a word. We can call this process the iconography of the mind, and it's automatic — not requiring conscious thought.

As each new word enters the mind, the process repeats. The mind will know if the word is an object, a connector or an action, automatically through its mental processing faculties. The basics of grammar and speech distill into these three primary categories:

1. Object - Nouns/pronouns and adjectives that modify or describe the quality of nouns.
2. Connector - This is a preposition, where a word indicates the relationship of the object in relation to another word or object.
3. Action - Verbs and adverbs that describe what an object is doing.

Now, continuing with the example poem, let's focus on the next word in the first line. Pain. Everyone has experienced pain – both physical and emotional. Your mind will remember different levels of pain and based on the next lines of the poem will know what type of pain you have experienced to associate with it. At this point in the poem, the pain is unknown because it's not clear what kind of pain the narrator is describing.

Also, there is a third hidden object in the first line. Did you pick up on it?

It's a combination of three words, "window of pain." Is it a window where the pain is seen through or a typical window pane of glass?

Now, because pain and pane sound phonetically the same, the mind associates it as the same word and automatically looks up both meanings in its extensive word-image database. This slightly confuses the mind as the mind is unsure what meaning to attribute to this particular word – a double entendre.

As a poet, this lapse in understanding, this slight gap, allows me to penetrate into your mind even further.

The mind is made up of different layers. It has created these layers to protect itself from ill speech and malicious people. Anything the person doesn't want to associate with.

My duty as a poet and writer is to penetrate all the layers of your mind and help you understand what I've written. The beautiful thing is that your mind will create its understanding from my words based on your life experiences, but if I'm a master of my craft, then your understanding will be very close to what I meant.

Let's continue and examine the poem in more detail.

The next line reads "is a broken glass."

I'm now telling your mind that the window referenced in the first line is a glass window and it broke.

If you have an analytical mind, it might be asking: how did the glass break, or who broke the glass? Did the narrator break the glass or was he thrown through the window head first? That last question might be the inquisitive nature of an over-analytical mind, like mine, trying to dig deeper through fanatical thought.

Then comes, "a shattered mess."

This describes the broken glass in more detail and quickly your mind is altering its original static image of what it pictured the window to be. The state of the window has changed, where the glass it once held, is shattered in a mess.

In three brief lines, I've transformed your self-created image of the window into an entirely different state of form.

"I pick up the shards / sharp as knives."

These are the next two lines readers will see.

Within these two lines, I share with you the state of the glass pieces. Even if you don't know what a shard of glass is, your mind knows what a sharp knife is. These lines, when combined in succession, get your mind to associate shards of glass with sharp knives.

Then, "I cut myself."

In three words, the narrator reveals a self-destructive nature. Some people who have experienced deep emotional pain and depression may have acted upon their negative thoughts and took action to harm themselves. These people are labeled "cutters" — those who cut into the flesh of their own body. It is not done with the specific intention to harm, but the physical pain lessens the emotional and mental turmoil, which brings us to the next line: "to numb the pain."

Quickly, the mind goes back to the first line, where we identify the experience of pain. I wrote the first line, in passing, without describing the pain in detail or indicating why the narrator was in pain. Now, we come full circle, looping back to the pain. This line also tells us why the narrator cuts himself in the previous line. Something else hurts much worse than the bite of the glass cutting through the skin.

Yet, the mind wants to know more. It's already deeply invested in discovering why there was a pain in the first place. What caused the pain?

As the poet and narrator, I answer that very question in the final two lines. "The pain / of losing you."

Is the poem really about you? Probably not, unless you were a woman I once loved and lost over a crumbling relationship. However, the "you" makes it deeply personal, a first person account of what happened. It's like I'm speaking directly to you, so this further embeds the meaning of the words in your mind. The poem is fully anchored in you now, and you can't ignore what I've written.

With the full meaning of the poem, your mind starts to associate past experiences of personal loss of a loved one. Perhaps it was an ex-girlfriend or ex-boyfriend who left you or a family member that suddenly died. Your mind will automatically find the most suitable life event from your past and relate to the entirety of the poem based on that single event.

The purpose of a great storyteller is to bypass the conscious mind and embed those words in the subconscious mind of the audience. When the reader or listener doesn't have to consciously think about the meaning, where it happens naturally as an extension of the process of how the mind works instead, then the story poem is more enjoyable. Yes, you can enjoy dark poetry too. I'm sure you have, by being able to relate to this poem.

To recap, here is a list of all the keywords or phrases in the poem, "Window of Pain":

Window
Pain
Window of pain
Broken glass
Shattered mess
Shards
Sharp (as) knives
Cut
Numb
Losing you

When we look at this list, reading each word slowly, our mind visualizes an image for each word. It is a natural process that takes years of specific training to stop, which most people do not have.

The final item on the list, "losing you" might not seem like an object, but it is. The mind may associate "losing you" with a person — a lost lover — who turns their back and walks away, never to return again. The word losing is both a verb and adjective. As a verb, it describes the loss of the person, but as an adjective, it emphasizes that suffering.

Here is a trick of the mind, it never sees the effect of the object separate from the object. So, if a man is running, it transforms into the language as the noun and verb, but the mind only sees it as a running man. There is no separating the object from its action because, from a holistic perspective, the effect cannot exist without that object.

Hopefully, after reading this essay on the theory of poetry and psychology, you have come to understand the importance of words in poetry, and even, in storytelling. After all, good poems tell a story.

But yet, that is not the entirety of what happened. This example poem is structured in a way to build upon the last sentence as your eyes cascade down the single stanza. What do I mean by this?

Each line in the poem is a stage of the story – slowly revealing the full spectrum of what the narrator knows. Edgar Allan Poe was a master of cascading, where each sentence flows into the next, further describing an event or thing or character's emotion. Poe's short story, "Tell-Tale Heart," is an excellent example of cascading.

If you haven't read it yet or haven't read it for

some time, I highly recommend it.

Cascading is a powerful storytelling technique, and I believe all great poets use it in one way or another. Maybe they don't use it line after line, but perhaps from verse to verse. Regardless, these masters of poetry — no, these masters of the written word — can connect important objects with other words as the poem unfolds.

The power of cascading executed properly by a master poet can drive home the meaning and emotion behind the words, letting those words more easily bypass the conscious mind and implant themselves into the subconscious. Once the subconscious mind takes hold of the phrase, it allows the unconscious mind to process it. The unconscious mind looks to see what the word means and what objects from the person's experience most closely relates to the word.

The words of a writer connect with the understanding of the reader. It is a highly significant relationship — a relationship of synergy and beauty. Without the reader, there would only be an audience of one, that of the writer who re-reads his works.

Without you — the reader — the purpose of my life would be unfulfilled.

A New Style of Poetry is Born

In 2017, after writing poetry for over two decades of my life, I formulated a new style of poetry. This new style I call *Versi D'oro*, which is to say in the Italian language, "The Golden Verse."

Before I explain the premise, theory, and rules of this new style, I would like to share with you a handful of poems composed in the style. After its invention, these are the six original poems I wrote:

Versi D'oro #1

This anticipation crawls
over ghostly skin
into the madness I descend.

Versi D'oro #2

A brown dog jumps, chasing birds
and he flees from bees
while sunshine dances on plum trees.

Versi D'oro #3

Life is but a lucid dream
with clocks ticking tocks
moving steadily as it mocks.

Versi D'oro #4

There is a voice inside me
where a raven speaks —
in silence, I grow deathly weak.

Versi D'oro #5

Her ethereal beauty
styled her as a queen —
Egyptian theatre of dreams.

Versi D'oro #6

Never stop your exploring —
these wonders of God
hide below the faces of sod.

The foundation of this style of poetry came about as an experiment. I was challenging myself to see if it was possible to create a poem that mathematically contained a portion of the Fibonacci sequence, using the count of syllables to represent the numerical values. Fibonacci is a sequence of numbers that starts with 1, 1, 2, 3, 5, 8, 13, 21 and 34. The pattern carries on indefinitely in this sequence for infinite.

The Fibonacci sequence is unique, because a new number in the string is equal to the two previous numbers. If we dive into the sequence shown above: take the number 5 and number 8, then add those two numbers together and the result is 13. The same mathematical principle is applied to any two numbers in the sequence, always resulting in a value equal to those numbers immediately preceding it.

Now, the Fibonacci sequence is interconnected to the golden ratio, because it follows the same mathematical principle.

An example from geometry reveals we have a large rectangle – the Golden Rectangle – that is formed by two disproportional shapes: Shape A, which is a large square, and Shape B, a medium rectangle. Shape B is smaller than Shape A, as it can fit within the other shape. The sides of Shape A are approximately 1.618 times longer in length than the sides of Shape B. This ratio is represented by the

Greek letter Phi, and is directly related to the Fibonacci sequence.

Definition of Golden Ratio

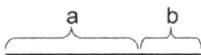

$$\text{Golden Ratio} = \frac{a+b}{a} = \frac{a}{b} = 1.61803 \text{ (approx)}$$

E.g. a "golden rectangle":

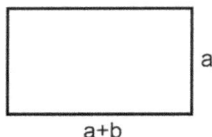

Many great works of art were formed from applying this technique, as it is evident in its skillful application by masterful artists and architects. Famous creative spirits who used the golden ratio in their art include Leonardo da Vinci, José Villagrán García, Ludwig Mies van der Rohe, and Le Corbusier.

I wanted to apply this same principle to poetry, but not in the same way Gregory K. Pincus did when he created the Fibonacci poetry style.

First off, if you ever read a poem in this style, you'll soon discover how disproportionate it looks as your eyes scroll down the page. It doesn't look pleasing or beautiful to the eyes. Even though I applaud Pincus for his creative efforts, it doesn't respect the space around the words.

The Fibonacci poetry style dictates that the first line must have 1 syllable along with the second line, followed with 2 syllables on the third line, 3 syllables on the fourth, 5 syllables for the fifth, and finally, 8 syllables on the sixth line. Visually, this creates a single stanza that grows line by line down the page.

Instead, I created a 3-line stanza poem that contained 7 syllables on the first line, 5 syllables on the second, and 8 syllables on the third. I was faced with the challenge to make the poem appear as if it was a formal style and also adhere to the mathematical principle that governs the golden ratio. It was not until I saw this image that it dawned on me how to formulate the style.

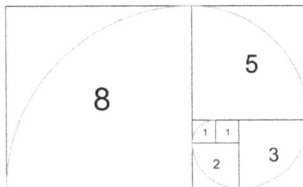

In the image, you see the first six numbers (1, 1, 2, 3, 5, 8) of the Fibonacci sequence. If we were to remove all the borderlines, we would be left with a large rectangle shape. The first four numbers in the sequence are all contained within the bottom right area of this large rectangle.

The numbers themselves correspond to the squared size of the shape (i.e. square inch, square foot). The next shape in the outward rotating spiral path is equal to the square sizes of the two shapes that preceded it. For example, the largest squared shape, which is labeled with the number 8 is equal in numerical value to the combined sizes of shapes number 5 and 3.

I used this geometrical sequencing as a guiding principle to determine and arrange the lines and their syllables in the Versi D'oro poetry style.

The shapes labeled with 1, 1, 2, 3 visibly compose themselves in a small rectangle shape in the bottom right section. When the numbers are added together the value equals 7. The square shape labeled with the number 5, in the upper right section, stands alone. As does the shape numbered with 8, which takes up the left side of the image.

We now have the numbers of 7-5-8 as the stand alone values. These values of 7-5-8 correspond to the syllable count for each of the three lines in this new style of poetic form.

I will leave you with one last example. A poem that highlights the fight between good and evil:

Versi D'oro #7.

Devils gnaw my pliant flesh
To test my spirit —
An angel whispers in my ear.

Suggested Reading

Listed in order of publication date.

"Secret Writing" (1841)
   Edgar Allan Poe

"The Philosophy of Composition" (1846)
   Edgar Allan Poe

"The Poetic Principle" (1850)
   Edgar Allan Poe

"A Poetry Handbook" (1994)
   Mary Oliver

"On Writing: A Memoir of the Craft" (2000)
   Stephen King

"The Art of Seduction" (2001)
   Robert Greene

"Lexicon" (2013)
   Max Barry

"Poetic Meter and Form" (2016)
   Octavia Wynne

"On Poetry" (2016)
   Glyn Maxwell

ABOUT THE AUTHOR, IN HIS OWN WORDS

This manifesto would not be complete unless you had some idea of who I am and the origins of my background.

The year was 1979, and the musical play "Sweeney Todd" debuted on Broadway. Two days later, on the other coast, I was born in Orange, California, and given the legal birth name of John Paul Hopkins. It would not be until my 30s that I would adopt the pen name of Alexander Bentley.

For many years my mother lived in the heart of Hollywood, where she put up with an unhappy marriage to my father. They often got into verbal and sometimes physical fights. I wasn't even one year old when my mom grabbed all our worldly possessions and fled in the middle of the night. After that night, I would never see my father again.

Once the ugly battle between my parents was over and ended in divorce, my mother took me and we traveled first to San Diego, California, then later to Phoenix, Arizona. It was the place I would grow up in as a child and where I spent most of my adult life.

I can honestly say I am beyond grateful for my mother, because she is the one person who had the patience to teach me how to read. The first, of two, kindergarten teachers, told my mom cruelly that I would never learn to read, that I would remain illiterate my entire life.

The teacher's opinion greatly upset my mother, so she set out to teach me how to read, by spending time with me every school night. We would pass the little booklets, back and forth. At first, she would read a few paragraphs, then let me read a few. During my year of kindergarten, I ended up reading 100 of those booklets for class.

Because of my mother, I am able to read. And reading has allowed me to become the writer and poet I am becoming today!

Before you close the pages of this book, I want to share one more personal story, which I hope gives you a deeper understanding of where I've been.

When my family and I were coming home from vacation, as we traveled through the Rocky Mountains in Colorado, a Jeep crashed into our van. I was asleep in the back, in a lawn chair, that wasn't strapped down. I had no seatbelt either, but somehow, miraculously I walked away from the accident without a scratch on my little body.

As lucky as I was, my step-father and my mother weren't. My step-father broke his left forearm, which required surgery and a steel plate embedded in his arm. My mother had her knee severely damaged, which also required extensive surgery. The damage was so severe my mom was practically immobile for several months.

If it wasn't for my step-father, then we may have died in that accident, all due to a head-on collision. But his split second decision and his swift move to steer the front of the van away from the oncoming Jeep saved our lives. He ended up taking the brunt of the force, as the other vehicle crashed into the driver's side.

Although my mom and step-dad would later divorce, he is forever in my memories, for the courageous act that saved my life.

UNDERWATER CHARADES[1]

You can write pretty little words
and put them down on paper
Roll that motherfucker up
into a beautiful scroll with angel wings
Send it off into the big wide open
world in a sky full of blue
But what depth does your writing possess
if you pen fancy quotes and dainty words?
Why keep your writings at the surface,
only showing a small glimpse of your character?
You're not a manufactured cliché
in a Hollywood plot, moving on a silver screen
But I see you as a living and breathing
human being, brooding in your skin
I want you — poets and vagabond
spirits, the troublemakers
To delve into lands of unknown emotion,
exploring the full capacity of your psyche

And come back with sand caked into
your wounds and a real story to share
A story that was both exhilarating and
exhausting to live in gritty and grainy technicolor
Don't just show me your pretty little jewels
you found on some beaten path
The leftovers that pedestrians looked over
or threw back to the dirty ground
Show me the horrible terrors you find deep
in the cave of your tortured soul
In a far off land that so few people know
Make me feel the scars living in your veins,
where the bad memories get buried but breathe
Show me all the fragile and broken
pieces that make you whole
Give me a reason to keep on reading,
then hit me with a truth so bold
it permanently seeps into my brain.

---

[1] Title suggested by poet and Colorado native, Linzi Pressley.

www.ingramcontent.com/pod-product-compliance
Lightning Source LLC
Chambersburg PA
CBHW061146040426
42445CB00013B/1584